Quaker Guns

CAROLINE KNOX

Quaker
Guns

WAVE BOOKS

Seattle & New York

Published by Wave Books

www.wavepoetry.com

Wave Books titles are distributed to the trade by

Consortium Book Sales and Distribution

Phone: 800-283-3572 / SAN 631-760X

Library of Congress Cataloging-in-Publication Data

Knox, Caroline.

Quaker guns / Caroline Knox. — 1st ed.

p. cm.

ISBN 978-1-933517-28-5 (alk. paper) —

ISBN 978-1-933517-27-8 (trade pbk. : alk. paper)

I. Title.

PS3561.N686Q83 2008

811'.54—dc22

2007037148

Designed and composed by Quemadura

Printed in the United States of America

9 8 7 6 5 4 3 2 1

FIRST EDITION

Wave Books 013

CONTENTS

Quaker Guns

DRESS PATTERN WITH AN INTERIOR

I will be assembled out of
noisy ecru tissue paper
printed with navy blue directions.
"Peace has the human dress."

Baste sensible Pellon along upper edge, dummy,
through all thicknesses, as shown;
raw edges even, pinking gusset and peplum.

Viyella is pinned to my components.
Topstitching takes place.
Now I am snappy Aunt Sally.

The contours gleam in the princess line, as I live and breathe.
In completion, seams get the Hong Kong finish,
a couture touch, and actually quite easy to do.

almost bolt upright in bed, not awake,
in the middle of the night
in about 1962, saying something like,
"Carol, Carol, they've found the statue."

"What statue?" I was almost awake. "The statue of Mary."
"Where?" "Buried underground."
I wanted to know more. "What is it made of? Marble?"
"It's made of foam rubber. They're
filling it with water to see what it weighs."

I wanted to know more. Mary is hidden in Amaryllis
as Amaryllis is hidden in vermiculite
in a red clay pot, buried.
What weight would you give to this.

After my brother's wedding in exactly 2000,
our entire family climbed up on the granite plinth
of the bronze statue of William Lloyd Garrison and just sat there
in bright day on Commonwealth Avenue.

My school friend Annie
is descended from Garrison,
so Garrison is hidden in Annie

as mica is hidden in vermiculite.
Garrison famously said, "I will be heard."
What weight would you give to this.
Do you want to know more.

Where would you dig. What would you find.

Bouki fait gumbo,
Lapin mangé li.

Bouki ▸ Wolof for hyena;
Verbs are French: *fait, mangé.*

Gumbo ▸ Native American or Bangena
= Okra = filé = "dried powdered young sassafras leaves,

discovered by the Choctaw Indians,"
says Miriam Knopf in *Around America:*
A Cookbook for Young People.

Compair Bouki, Compair Lapin =
Brer Fox and Brer Rabbit.

"The hyena may have made the gumbo,
but it's the rabbit that ate it"—a distich of power
and viable Marxist grumbling?

Compair Aesop fait (get Greek word for "tale")
Compair LaFontaine fait fable.
God gives, but He doesn't share.

Compair Aesop fait fable.
Compair LaFontaine mangé Aesop.

Even gumbo z'herbes in a starving time, desperate cooking, meager soup.

Compair Marianne Moore traduit LaFontaine,
Compair Joel Chandler Harris fait storybook,
Choctaw Indians mangé gumbo.

WE BEHELD TWO NEBULAS:

first, the nebula Midges, a diffuse
nebula, and like all diffuse
nebulas, a luging blob

wheeling light, the starry map
of cells which die every day,
of seed-shaped clay molecules;

these were atomized rotor-thrown
specks pocking a fresco—
a marks and sparks assay

in spume made out of rays
and friable ice slivers spot on;
a shower with half-life

dapple and shadow, but no pepper.
Not pellet but mote, messier
dust where lights had been

and next to shard-dust lights again.
But then came porous borders
osmosis as from lake to sky—

volatile horse sneezes, froth and pollen flecks,
aerosol scintillas, spores, plush winged burrs,
chatto and windus, forked nettles:

like the time-release decorative arts
conservative and retardataire
bands of egg-and-dart, bands of

acanthus leaf, bands of fronds,
mop-tops and lace-caps
in slo-mo sediment in space.

And through vertiginous time
the fibrous cysts were dispelled
in a spot compression

not unlike the components
of a bruise or of the pox chickenorum, ether/ore.
Shafts of powder shunted downward.

The pathology was dot-matrix, you see.
And we also beheld the nebula Smoke,
a planetary nebula (like all planetary

nebulas, nothing at all to do with planets):
well-defined disks, reductive space-junk really—
frisbees and outdoorsy tin can lids

—you know, the atmospherics, "so bright a unit"—
operational CDs and DVDs.
Serious pizzas. Subway tokens, 45s,

slugs, medallions, aspirin, contact lenses,
scrap klister, specie (parts and labor).
Oh yes—we beheld these two nebulas in a fictograph,
nebula Midges and nebula Smoke.

MY ANORAK

I put on my anorak
and a CD of Dvorak.

A Jesuit
appeared in an apesuit.

Rubbing his sunburn with aloe
vera, he joined the BPOE.

Next time I saw him was in Tacoma
lecturing on the pueblo at Acoma,
a statelier
atelier.

QUAKER GUNS

Your handsome workmanlike fourmaster,
out on a reach, no sight of land,
mirrors the adventure tales for children and grownups—oh, isn't the brightwork
bright; oh, the cannon royal, the twenty-four pounders.
It's safe to assume that you have eighty-six guns.

But these aren't worth the powder
it takes to blow them to hell.
Shipmasters long ago thought up this protection.

They're Quaker guns, a creative ruse, the kind you couldn't and wouldn't
fire: they're flotsam, jetsam, or any old trees, ships' logs.
They're broken masts. They're the Friends of the Friends.
These logs are laid in the loading trays—
you have twelve cannon at most, but they look like an armada.
So privateers mistake the logs for guns, and scarper,
afraid of driftwood posing as ordnance.
No pirate would go anywhere near you.

ANDIRONS

I wanted to make a pair of andirons
for our fireplace, so I pulled down the copper
gutters along the eaves, which I boiled up
with some brass doorknobs and tin cans. Soon
there was a scary and roiling mixture,
an alloy for my project. I put in my zinc pills and my iron ones.
I put in some silver earrings and a gold-plated tie-pin
in the shape of a lyre. I stirred this all around.
The metal combers came and went
like Philippe-Auguste Villiers de L'Isle-Adam, like Nicolas Restif de la Bretonne.

A voice spoke out of the gleaming depths.
"I am the copper gutters who were wont to protect
your house and yard from torrents and to make it look nice.
I am the useful brass doorknobs who led you into the dining room
and the bedroom and the kitchen. I am the tuna
and chili bean holders, tin cans; I am the Medaglia D'Oro cans
whose contents woke you and kept you going. I am the zinc pills
that strengthened you, along with the iron pills which I also am,
and the earrings, I am the earrings, which although ugly are made of silver
and came from deep in the earth, perhaps from Cuzco. I am the tie-pin,
most important of all, I am the tie-pin in the shape of the lyre,
and who are you to look down on me, you who are meant to be a poet but who
    are acting like an idiot,

you who know that the lyre is the instrument of Apollo and the symbol of
   what poets do all day every day.
I am the voice of these substances speaking to you out of the gleaming depths,
soon to become andirons with welded billet bars, meat racks, upturned feet,
   and scrolled tops decorated with geometric chiseling."

The poem begins all wrong in medias res
so it looks like a fragment, a throwaway,
something that goes nowhere—you'd be
embarrassed to have it read. The poem
has no subject or imagery system. You
couldn't call it coherent. But still

THE TITLE

was and is here, down in the middle of the
poem, halfway down the page instead of at
the expected centered top margin so that
when the end of the poem finally comes there's
enough at the top and bottom of the page
to constitute something to do, it is something to do.

DREYKEN

Dreyken fabe, wer ingete dreyken
(dor droy rittavittastee orn canar).
Preb. Refen ingete inget. Preb.

Santona nofa Xeroc;
ter quittz mivin movip.
Morm faria greel Florida
faria greel pandeck.

BATHROBES

We took our bathrobes and stuck them in the washer.
(Ritta put hers in the blue laundry machine.)
I said, "Refen ingete inget."

Nocturnes are hard to Xerox;
birds follow the glare of water.
We prepare tax returns for people in Florida,
people in Florida whom we have never met.

(Translated by the author and Caroline Knox)

15

"If you love the house, you also love the crow on the roof,"
    goes the proverb in this part of the world.
    What is the painted design around the doors
    of significant spaces in the southerly part
    of Yin Yu Tang, a Chinese merchant's house
    from the eighteenth century, a place of toil and gifts

for the Huang family, a place of red carp, of gifts
    of thanks for prosperity that falls through the roof
    skywells, into the carp pools of the house?
    The black and white designs lead to the world
    of the house, and of the house's part
    in shade and shelter, screens, staircases, doors.

"The snow will bring the world indoors,"
    says Sean O'Brien in "Blizzard," one of the gifts
    of reading the TLS, the poetry part,
    in ink with the luster of lacquer, a poem for the roof,
    on paper that glows, the palest in the world.
    Snow is tracked and trampled in the merchant's house.

The weather falls abundantly to the pools in the house
    through preindustrial framing techniques around the doors
    (the path of the wood grain, either straight or whorled,

decides the use of a beam). For food as gifts,
red carp wait in pools below the roof;
screens open and close between part and part.

Some incremental repetition, a part
of the architecture: "If you love the house,
you also love the crow," says the proverb, "on the roof."
The family present the gifts before the doors;
the honorable ancestors receive the family's gifts.
I keep hearing "Blizzard"—"The snow will bring the world

indoors"—it will fall through the skywells of the world
melting by the carp in the significant part
of Yin Yu Tang in the plenty of its gifts.
The painted design in black and white on the house
mimics the costlier carvings on walls and doors
of ancient places, mimics the black crow on the roof.

        The roof of the world
        is China; the tall doors part
        in the house of gifts.

IT WAS CHRISTMAS

It was Christmas, and I was stuck
wrapping fungible musk potions for chums,

but there was no snow except fake in stores
where I purchased the above and the sparkly.

"Nature in awe to Him/Hath doff'd her gaudy trim" about covers it.
Yet then snowflakes, building on two basal facets and six prism facets,
    began to fall, and next

rain mashed down all the last leaves into Wheaties.
This humectant rain we could have used in August.

—Wrapping bottled potions in first tissue paper and then
giftie boxes, foil. "God hath made the stars the foil," you know,

suitable for the snazzy dominical present. Wrapping potions
for beloved chums in all zones, actually,

and lashing the boxes with elastic tinsel cord, the wrap outlay
costing in some cases more than the gift. We live in Zone 6,

according to the Wayside Catalog. *Franklinia* and *Stewartia* can flourish here
if protected. Bartram found *Franklinia*

and named it after duh Franklin; species *alatamaha,*
from the Indian tribe and river. When Bartram

went back for more, the trees were gone. We are protected
in Zone 6 enough to make these treasure trees bloom

alongside of the "junipers shagged with ice"
where chums, co-monotheists and/or doubters get the absolute adjective,
    the sparkly.

HOOKE'S LAW

1. SLEEK TRIP

The poem was a ticket.
It was a flimsy
transfer to the Silver Line
at South Station. At the ICA,
the Institute of Contemporary Art,
we cantilevered over the
harbor, what choice did we have?
In the theater the backdrop
was tugs barges cranes.
It was the world.

2. TOWN SIGN

Dedham, Massachusetts, was in the
17thC called Contentment. Here
notably were Sacco and Vanzetti
tried. Here throve Dedham Pottery,
a light in the Boston Arts
and Crafts movement. Here
lived and painted
Philip Leslie Hale and

Lilian Westcott. Here
lived Diane Wald and Arielle
Greenberg, writing books of poems.
This sign is for them all.

3. A VEILED VOICE SPOKE:

"It's basic Martin Buber—I
don't want to see Thou, me; Thou
dostn't want to see
Moi. I'll bet a cool thou
it's right there in the
John Adams (▸Locke) (▸Grotius)
Bill of Rights—you don't
have to have anyone
over you don't want to."

The veiled voice went mute.

4. IBM

"They've invented a machine
that will do your work for you.
Everyone laughs at it, but
I'm going to buy a lot of
shares. They cost almost
nothing. I think the machine

will do our work for us." It's
1946, '48, the New Look:
Dior, Paris, city of
light and exile, where
Russian poems get written.

5. ELIZABETH,

may I introduce my friend
Arnold Arboretum? Arnold,
this is Elizabeth New Jersey.
Now here is Howard, Howard
University—Arnold, Elizabeth,
this is Howard. Here is Pierre,
my friend Pierre South Dakota,
you haven't met. You haven't
met Mariana Trench. Mariana,
come on, come over here by this
cartload of martinis, and say hello to
Arnold, Pierre, Howard, Elizabeth.

6. BOOK

The book you are reading,
Quaker Guns, contains the
sequence you are reading,
two sonnets, two haiku,

a sestina, an homage
to George Herbert, some tercets,
a masque, two translations,
two erasure poems, an elegy,
a recipe, a song, an ABC,
an eclogue, a canzone,
a group of rubayyat, and other poems.

7. TALON

European advances in aero-
dynamics mean that the Talon
bullet is covered with black
Lubalox. The bullet has a controlled
expansion upon target impact.
It has been demonized. There are
implications for the wounded.
Check it out on elk! There is
always more to learn. Odi
et ammo, that's what I say.

8. YOUR BLOOD

Your blood flows through
your veins and even capillaries,
around and across you, like
the Eisenhower Gold Star Highway System.

Your blood, everybody's blood
cleans itself and adjusts
its components like the
overt torment of a sandlot
percussion and vocal
trio singing and playing
SHAKA SHAKA SHAKA
DON'T FORGET YOUR SHAKA
THAT IS IT   I LOVE IT

9. CHEESE ARGUMENT

You could make a meal
of it: GORGONs would
snap it up: Piave, Brie,
Boucherondin, at the
milk and honey bazaar.
Stilton, Cheshire,
Chaume, Camembert,
Harpies would snap them up,
a meal for Émile ZOLA.

10. HOOKE'S LAW

"You're the elastic limit," we were told,
and with reason. Hooke's Law
states that within the limit,

strain is proportional to stress.
All solids are elastic, but beyond
the limit, certain dents occur.
A pioneer in physics and in math,
optics, watchmaking, Robert Hooke,
Fellow of the Royal Society,
singlehandedly he invented the term *cell*.

WHO'LL BUY

Who'll buy my plus fours,
come buy my petits fours.
Hark high and disposedly to my set piece,
come buy my rose grosgrain *étuis*.

Who'll buy my silicone shuttlecocks, dishwasher safe?
Is your teapot Shardsville?

Come buy my rebuilt Super Rebel Airplane Kit
with docile stall characteristics
and retrofit fuselage utilizing
a semi-monocoque construction.
Who's to say if this is any improvement?
It depends what you like.

Are you having trouble about an
internal combustion engine with
a MacPherson-strut-type design?
Have you got a swickle tranny?

LINE POEM

Long jetty, long shell-racked jetty, cracked warped planks.

Beautiful fish, beautiful sea-bass poached with an August tomato, on an
    ironstone plate.

A snake's slough, a snake's spinal cord, a dry-rot stump.

A twill tape measure, an audiotape cassette unspooled and puckered, shining.

Agate prayer beads, kazoos, whistles, rattles.

A bike chain and a bungee cord. A möbius strip and a broccoli elastic.

Split vanilla pod inset with paltry-looking flat oily brown seeds.

Egg-and-dart molding of vitreous fake sandstone. Contrails, mares' tails,
    mackerel sky.

At ten after five, we pulled up carrots between green
beans. "How many times the poem contains vegetables! and mountains
of thy remembrance, so to speak," sings the flinger of carrot and bean seed.
He surprises with refrain of an old song as he flings the seeds
of unreasoning summer. They germinate in fire, growing beyond red rivers
that, by responding to carrot tops of fair perpetual
ways cloaked with renewal and to bean vines ten feet the least length, flow;
"my body turns toward tops and vines as sinuous as

thee," intones the flinger of seed. A veggie riot
again photosynthesized, for the stars have been kind to the plants. The bean
    vine is not
finished in the nobler trees, and the carrot tops know
the language of leaves repeats flashing greenery.
The flinger of seed is to us a bacchant. He cries

with eventual perfection, while west deserves of dusk,
while east deserves of dawn. He cries among flowers partedpetaled:
"i lie at length, breathing with my mouth, face as a cognate of vegetables,
with shut eyes, contemplating the bean and carrot, so delirious. It's indivisible,
the total experience, and is an example of prevenient grace,
the sweet earth where thou liest,
as photosynthesis is an example of dancing."

"Source Text" is a poem that deliberately appears to be a source text from which E. E. Cummings could have written as erasure poems "Song VI" and "Song VII" (from XLI Poems [1925] in *Complete Poems 1913–1962*, New York 1972, 184–185), below:

SONG VI

after five
times the poem
of thy remembrance
surprises with refrain

of unreasoning summer
that by responding
ways cloaked with renewal
my body turns toward

thee
again   for the stars have been
finished in the nobler trees and
the language of leaves repeats

eventual perfection
while east deserves of dawn.
i lie at length, breathing
with shut eyes

the sweet earth where thou liest

SONG VII

between green
                  mountains
sings the flinger
of

fire   beyond red rivers
of fair perpetual
feet the
sinuous

              riot

the
flashing
bacchant.

partedpetaled
mouth, face
delirious.   indivisible
grace

      of dancing

COORDINATES

He craved potassium, so he drank V8.
His Smith-Corona was an Olivetti,
a toboggan with a green and silver keyboard.

Einstein was from Ulm, and Abraham from Ur.
We folded our laundry in the Pyrenees
Mountains. She looked at biota on the seaboard.

They ransacked the sofa for the coins inside.
I rinsed my hair; he ate some grits;
you kissed him in the arbor, so he fed her cat

on quindim de yayá, a custard dessert.
In shoes that made noise, we sang at the Ritz
the Buxtehude *Magnificat*.

She will teach crafts at Gondola University
until he gazes at the Italy of memory.
We will indulge ourselves at the Sert

Café, yet he will envy your swine.
You loved my hat, but they emailed his bride
a rain of virtual confetti.

They loved her with all our heart;
he loved them with all my book.
She said her name was Crêche Mangerhay.

Here is something you can substantiate:
these are nonce tercets; every line
rhymes with another somewhere or other.

You carded the wool and he praised the sheep.
The osprey is mousing and frogging in the swamp.
He will not sample the marshmallow peep.

THE OWL AND THE LARK

LARK

You wouldn't be one of those Vermiculated Fishing-owls, would you?
   from Africa?
or a Tengmalm's Owl? "Hark hark the lark," you snored, the remote light
and/or caffeine resetting the circadian rhythms of the clock. You're such
   a hoot.

OWL

Why can't I find the circadian rhythms of the remote—
it's phosphorescent, why can't I find the remote, oh you who are
named after a discontinued GM car?

LARK

So sorry to disturb your dirigible ad rem sleep patterns, you who are
distinguished by subtle markings (to wit, gray facial discs) as you utter
   horned sones from the barn sofa,
but if you can't keep track of the remote, do you even deserve to watch

reruns of Green Acres? Especially the one where they don't know they
   have to crack the eggs open
to cook them? I thought you were supposed to be a wise old authority
   on Nature.

OWL

Nature is the red slayer, wrote Emerson in 1862. And anyway, it's reruns
   of Mr. Ed, not Green Acres,

and of WKRP, that I admire. WKRP has the best theme song
of any TV show ever. What makes you think I'm from Africa?

LARK

Emerson wasn't talking about Nature as the red slayer, he was talking about
    Wampanoags. Caffeine is a more reliable obsession
than reruns. In caffeine's wand, you soar in daydreams, down clouds
    of down.

OWL

I flew over Amsterdam last night, observing the white bicycles.
I soared at night on owl adrenaline, looking for mice in Delft.
The white bicycles belong to the city of Amsterdam.

LARK

Baby's Coffee in Key West is my best source for soaring.
Their finest cup is Voodoo Queen. That should be your dish of tea,
    nocturnal one.
What's with the white bicycles? I didn't say I thought you were from Africa.

OWL

The city owns them; if you need to get somewhere in Amsterdam,
    you take one,
and when you've gotten there, you leave the white bike
for someone else to use. —You made up Tengmalm's Owl.

LARK

Isn't "vermiculated" a disgusting word?

OWL

                                    Isn't the Oversoul a vague concept?

LARK

Maybe you threw the remote out the window
when you threw the toaster out the window during the Toaster Fire.

OWL

Maybe I didn't. Who is Tengmalm?

LARK

Come to find out, he's a Swedish naturalist.
Caffeine makes you feel phosphorescent, actually,
like the remote you don't seem to be able to find.

OWL

The barn sofa needs to be reupholstered, actually,
with down, fabulous down. Maybe then
I'll find a lot of quarters and the phosphorescent remote.

LARK

Last night I nested in destructive phragmites.
Why can't they harvest it, and make rugs or beer?
But see now how the moon is daunted by solar glare in a cross-eyed aubade!

OWL

Now the day begins, and we return to ordinary birdhood,
from our literary appointments as tropes of human predilections!

Oh, hearts, bells, leaves, acorns.
Oh, swords, bells, cups, money.

Oh, hearts (*coeur*).
Oh, clubs (*tréfle*).
Oh, spades (*pique*); mystery—oh, Sam Spade.
Oh, diamonds (*carreau*), oh, John Le Carré; oh, Neil Diamond.

Oh, animals, flowers, human figures.

Oh, hold the austere diamond against the windowpane.
The King, Queen, and Jack in their sandwich boards believe you are waving.
No, you are scratching a message with texture and content.
Oh, *tréfle* (trefoil)—they have returned from the club, the Trefoil Club.
Oh, swords! The King carries them.
Shallow blond Jack's emblem is the mystery herb.

Oh, animals, flowers, human figures:
like animal, eland, "That's eland he's offering you" (Ernest Hemingway 1936).
Like flower, rose, city of thorns, Thornburgh, Dick Thornburgh,
    Attorney General under Reagan.
Like human figure? For I have a thorn in my side, and a foot in my mouth;

the lion has a thorn in his foot: I am Androcles with tweezers.
I have a club foot, I belong to the Foot Club. I belong to the Weed Club,
   I'm the President.

Oh, Dorothy Parker! oh, Dorothy Oh, a fine actor!

SALAD

1   Line a new shoe box with oiled waxed paper. Make up a batch of cranberry-banana Jell-O and chill; allow it to begin to jell. Finely grate a small head of red cabbage; fold it together with half a pound of currants and half a pound of shredded coconut into the jelling mixture. Carefully pour the mixture into the lined shoebox and allow to jell firmly.

2   In another bowl, make up a batch of lime Jell-O and chill; allow it to begin to jell. Shred six carrots and add them; add a cup of drained mandarin oranges and quarter of a cup of finely chopped chives. Carefully pour the mixture over the #1 layer without disturbing it.

3   In a third bowl, make up a batch of orange Jell-O and chill; allow it to begin to jell. Peel and chop four apples, Granny Smith and McIntosh, and six sticks of celery; chop half a cup of walnuts. Add these to the mixture, along with a package of rainbow baby marshmallows. Carefully pour the mixture over the #2 layer without disturbing it.

4   In a fourth bowl, make up a batch of strawberry Jell-O and chill; allow it to begin to jell. Chop finely a half pound each of dried dates and figs. Together with a cup of slivered almonds, add the dates and figs to the strawberry mixture. Carefully pour the mixture over the #3 layer without disturbing it.

5   In a fifth bowl, make up a batch of lemon Jell-O and chill; allow it to begin to jell. Add a half pint of cottage cheese, half a jar of Major Grey's chutney,

a package of alfalfa sprouts, and a package of Bac-Os. Carefully pour the mixture over the #4 layer without disturbing it.

6 In a sixth bowl, make up a batch of cherry Jell-O; allow it to begin to jell. Add a can of drained garbanzo beans, a can of drained kidney beans, and a half cup of crumbled feta cheese. Carefully pour the mixture over the #5 layer without disturbing it; finally, the shoebox should be full.

7 Allow the salad to jell overnight in the icebox. Just before serving time, invert the box onto a platter and peel off the waxed paper. Mask the salad with Cool Whip into which six tablespoons of Cointreau have been folded. Dust the top of the Cool Whip with cinnamon and nutmeg. Slice and serve.

before anyone else
comes to,
dude, my
eager
face pressed to the
glass house.
I think it's
just a
knockout
locution
minus
Nerf
opportunities,
photo ops of African animals, never
quiche.
Really,
see it his way:
"The ground holds too many shards," wrote T. H. Breen,
unaware of how right he was—who could be?
Virginia Woolf, maybe.
We couldn't tell what was really going on in the photograph of the
xebu, because of overexposure.
You see, we're in the Nerf quiche
zone again.

OLDEST DOG

My beloved old dog Cyrus
died at 15 years,
so I went out and bought
bird food and along came
Lardina, a mourning dove,
so named because of her
great girth. She scarfed up
all the food and wanted
more. Her friends came
too and soon I was
spending more on dove
food than on dog food
previously. Cyrus's friends
Wolfie and Oliver came
for a while looking for him.
Crisco, Lardina's boyfriend, came over.
Carpe canem, I wrote down, *Cave diem.*
Sic 'em, I told Lardina of the blue jays
every morning. Crisco is too large to move.
Oldest dog: when the vet said,
He's having trouble breathing,
I said, Shouldn't he be put
to sleep now? The vet said,
I'll do this as soon as you go out the door;
well, that's what we did.

NERF

A nameless child sings, and the song is set
in a quatrain by a passing and nameless poet,
who makes another quatrain and another
with "succinctness, spontaneity, and wit"

on the basis of the first, a poem made of Nerf,
safe and exciting, a synthetic surf.
Omar wrote such stanzas in the twelfth
century on tented desert turf.

He was *The Rubayyat's* august *auteur*
whose "gloomy quatrains" (so John Hollander)
enjoyed a vogue for centuries to come.
(Some were not by Omar, but most were.)

Nerf was invented back in '69
by Parker Brothers Games. It was divine.
Nerfman and Nerfball flew around the house
destroying nothing, everything was fine.

The photosynthetic sun is climbing high
in that inverted bowl we call the sky
above, which is as blue as any Smurf
consumerism used to opt for. I

read the WASP redaction by Edward Fitzgerald
(1859). He was a herald
of interest in Middle Eastern art,
in ignorance of which they stand imperiled

who have no clue what they're supposed to do
with Kaikobad the Great, or Kaikhosru.
My edition is illustrated by
the American Pre-Raphaelite Elihu

Vedder, of the stock of the patroon,
in 1894. It is maroon
with golden speckles and a padded cover.
Omar invokes the sands, the wind, the moon,

apocalyptic rubies, kisses, scars,
vessels of wine, of gaping earth, and stars.
These figure the death of monarchs and beautiful women,
tall as the cypress, intimate of wars.

Another singer sings, and it is not
Edward Fitzgerald, it's Ella; she is hot
and cool in every quatrain and in grand
abstracted syllables of scat like shot.

She makes a stanza of the blues for a ruba'i
a stanza of the blues for a ruba'i
oh why didn't I think of it oh why
a stanza of the blues for a ruba'i

Miss Fitzgerald's notable reserve
is overlaid with elegance and verve:
"Maybe it's because it's what I love to do—
The moment I hit the stage I get the nerve."

I packed up the books: *Under*
Milk Wood, Of
Mice and Men, Under
the Window, Under
the Volcano, Up
from Slavery, The Thunder-
ing Herd, Under
the Greenwood Tree, The Over-
Coat, The Changing Light at Sandover,
Under-
world, Out
of Africa, Paris Trout;

and I went over
to the Under-
woods' house over
on River Road. Over-
head the blackness of
clouds out-
paced a fleeing sun. Out
and up
the clouds rolled, roiled up,
wrung out
in horrendous rain over
and over.

I had agreed over
coffee one day to farm out
lots of books people were giving over
to the library book sale over
at the high school. Under
the agreement, volunteers took books over
to the Underwoods' over
spring break. I was up
for this, and signed up.
Over
I drove, up
the Cross Road, and turned up

River Road. I walked up
the Underwoods' driveway and over
the lawn. The voice of Dawn Up-
shaw drifted up
from a CD player, and out
on the screen porch was John Up-
dike's new book of essays, next to the Up-
anishads. Under
the lilacs, under
the clematis, climbing up
trellises of
lath, of

ironwork, of
wicker, blossoms hardly held up
their heads. Of
course, of

course; but the storm that had crushed them was over.
Pools of
water, of
mud were all around. The Underwoods' cookout
was a washout,
but the sun of
a glowing afternoon under-
cut the thunder.

The Under-
woods took all the discarded books out
of the trunk of my car, and then drove them (with lots of other books) over
to the high school, where these books were put up
for sale for the benefit of the Westport Free Public Library, a generous act
    which the Underwoods should be proud of.

TITLE LAW IS PLEASANT

I'm going to Italy
on Xanax Airlines.
I'm going to Pisa
to sojourn in a place.

Ogunquit is everywhere like Volendam
Volendam is everywhere like Ogunquit
O is like V
V is like O

The pilot is 1.59 meters tall
And weighs 60 kilos.

Title law is pleasant, as real estate is outdoors.
Be like Lance.
Be on a bike.
You be like Lance.

WIND TURBINE

Three blades, vanes, seventy-
seven feet across each one:
lose the oil, the oil is not
in it. Now hear this:
stash serious green lolly
by an exigent spindle
on a tapered tubular
steel tower, a unit of a
wind farm; it goes around like
Mozart goes around, he
who wrote "Twinkle Twinkle."
One hundred and sixty-four feet,
and tall with it, don't you know,
big time, large print, *mit luftpost.*

SPINOZA

In the shadows of the ghetto, the Jew's light hands
rub and rub his spectacles in the dying
afternoon. It's cold outdoors and the nights
are all like one another. But his hands lying
in his lap and polishing in space
and the pale spikes of hyacinth which stand
there hardly exist for him who dreams and dreams
and rubs awake the universe's maze.

       Fame, that dream in another dream's reflection
       doesn't afflict him nor can touch it seems
       any more than women his affection.
       Constantly as with myth and metaphor cast
       aside, the Jew rubs the lens that is the vast
       shining image of the one who is all his lights.

(Jorge Luis Borges, translated by Caroline Knox)

FACE-MASQUE

ONDINE

I am reading *The Waves*, by Virginia Woolf; I am reading *A Wave*, by John Ash-
bery. "The eyes are fissures of men."
(Who was Admiral Farragut?)

HAIBUN

Being shell, your whole driveway in the underwater world is rich in calcium.
This calls attention to its work. I will radio you across the salt rocks, with my
Wave radio in fact, nothing if not plastic. Now they make extrusive shoes
you can swim in, with grippers, so you don't slip and cut your feet; all the
rocks have slippery tar. "The eyes are fissures of men." Jane and I took the
dogs around the point through the drying September weeds—nine varieties
of goldenrod, and rosa rugosa with fruit and flowers on the same stem. A
gracious neighbor has caused a causeway to be made from beach to beach in
the crunchy undergrowth. There are metal detectors humming everywhere.
If only I could complete this statement in my round copperplate hand.

(Sealed like a limpet to the foregoing: Most protozoa, the one-celled animals,
are motile—amoeba, hydra, paramecia—with "unedited sense impres-
sions.")

ONDINE

The horse latitudes, calms near the Tropics of Cancer and Capricorn, are re-
gions of light, variable winds. In contrast to the doldrums, the air here is
fresh and clear. My Tristan!

TAR

My horse latitudes!

ASHBERY

Here's what the poet wrote there then, back in aught-84:
"I think all games and disciplines are contained here,
Painting as they go, dots and asterisks that
We force into meanings that don't concern us
And so leave us behind."

CRUSTACEAN

By maritime loran, by lo(ng) ra(nge) n(avigation)
I proceed, a L=A=N=G=U=A=G=E crustacean.

SCENERY

That girl needs rescuing out there in the boat
—her friend is back hysterical on the shore—
the former the girlfriend of that boyfriend of each
of whom it was observed this morning when we saw them hitch
but picked them not up, on the way to our boring aunt's
place up in Portsmouth, New Hampshire: these kids these days!
At their non-sectarian coed day and boar
ding school of rustic suburban rightish stance!
popping with rhetorical questions, afloat
in blancmange literally, or sinking in it, says:
          The wrong sestet hooked up with the right octave?
          Would I swallow that, hook line and sinker? Not wav
          ing but drowning (Stevie Smith) and yet
          remember the dryads are the ones who are never wet.

HAIBUN

My daughter went to stay with a girl who couldn't sail, but who took a windsurfer out in bad weather anyway. The girl got in nautical trouble immediately, of course. A grizzled coot on the beach said, in my daughter's hearing, "That girl needs rescuing out there in the boat. Her friend is back hysterical on the shore." My daughter heard two pentameters, ran and wrote them down on something, and brought them home.

As we know, Newton's particles of light are sand upon the red sea shore.

ONDINE
Tristan da Cunha!

TAR
Oil.

OIL
Tar.

TAR
Come all ye who would hear
a chantey of the sea.
My quatrains are reliable
so hearken unto me.

On hard tack and tobacco
we reckon we can thrive.
I've smoked a lot of Luckies
and I'm lucky to be alive

to cross the latitudes beneath
occluded stars and suns
where on the privateers
we train our Quaker guns.

Come to Tristan da Cunha
the overmythologized isles.
Travel west from Cape Town
several thousand miles

to where they speak the lonely dialect
and a lake sits high in the snow.
Come to Tristan da Cunha
the archipelago.

RHODA

I can think of my Armadas sailing. . . .

MARCEL

Wave.

CETACEAN

Scenery.

HAIBUN

News and Strange Newes from St. Christophers of a tempestuous Spirit, which is called by the Indians a *Hurry-Cano* or whirlewind, which hapneth in many of those Ilands of *America* or the *West-Indies*, as it did in *August* last, about the 5. day. 1638, blowing downe houses, tearing up trees by the *rootes*, and it did puffe men up *from the earthe, as they had beene Feathers, killing diverse men:* most of these miserable people were reduced to their first principles. The Hurry-Cano or Harricane (to the vulgar, Harry) is swayed or hurried with its own robustuous motion, or as the influences and force of the Planets doe drive it. "Harry is expected," they say. At this tyme, the edges of the clouds are guilded with various and frightening Colours, as a pale fire colour, next to that of a dull yallow, and nearer the Body of the Cloud, of a Copper Colour, terrible and amazing even beyond expression.

But Jane and I came home by the salt pond where the fish are born with no eyes, and can't live: "added concern with external nature."

MARCEL

Marceau.

CHARLES

Martel.

TAR

Gob.

GOB

Tar.

HAIBUN

The islanders on Tristan are 95 in number, as of 19-aught-9. They manage their own affairs without any written laws, the project once entertained of providing them with a formal constitution being deemed unnecessary. The inhabitants are described as moral, religious, hospitable to strangers, well mannered and industrious, healthy and long lived. They are without in-toxicating liquors and are said to commit no crimes. They are daring sailors, and in small canvas boats of their own building voyage to Nightingale and Inaccessible Islands. They knit garments from the wool of their sheep; are good carpenters and make serviceable carts. Tristan has a volcanic cone (7640 ft.) capped with snow but containing a fresh-water lake.

"On Tristan, we have this Tristan-slang." "Some whalers came over, mid-century, so we are somewhat Yankeefied."

SCENERY

Scenery.

ASHBERY

Lighting.

MAKEUP

Ondine.

PROPS

Pilings.

ONDINE

Like as the Waves, that branch of women's work
in World War II, so does the actual ocean,
in uniforms of navy blue and white.
A *Wave* made her write haibun.
I will interface with my human counterpart
at the See the Sea Motel in Weekapaug, Rhode Island.

GOTH PLAINT

O for a dripping steak, garlic,
all pierced like Sainte-Chapelle

on a charger onyx with a greige matrix, O
for a bombazine cloak the color of plankton!

"Quirinus, loosen up on the metheglin!
Dr. Jenner, Dr. Mesmer,
what about an infusion of spirits?"

Blessed Sycorax, pointed arches send the stress immediately into the ground.
Mad, eyeless fowl, the questioners ingest your guts.

NEWFOUNDLAND DOG EARS HAIKU

This beautiful big
black dog's innocent floppy
ears are like the rain.

ERASURE ERASURE

The

       YOUNG *Centaur*

                       was

                              To

select   a book;   we   approve

                   A good

                         number

       Handy;

           the intention;   his

       wiping out *rare*

    GIBBON

                 settle-

ments.

The source for this erasure poem is the OED entry for "erasure":

Erasure:
    The action of erasing or obliterating.
    1755 YOUNG *Centaur* vi. Wks. **1757** IV.277 The desperate
erasure of his Christian name. **1817 W. SELWYN** *Law Nisi
Prius* II. 825 The devise to the trustees was not revoked by
the erasure. **1836 J. GILBERT** *Chr. Atonem.* ii (1852) 31 To
select a part [of a book] which we happen to approve,
and by evasive arts to effect the erasure of the other part.
1851 MAY *Const. Hist.* (1863) I.i.24 The erasure of his
name from the list of privy councilors.
  b. An instance of erasing or obliterating.
    1734 tr. *Rollin's Anc. Hist.* (1827) I.ii.239 A good per-
formance is not to be expected without many erasures and
corrections. **1817 COLERIDGE** *Biog. Lit.* 183 If the number
of these fancied erasures did not startle him. **1858 LD. ST.
LEONARDS** *Handy Bk. Prop. Law* xix 146 The erasure was
not made by the testator with the intention to revoke his will.
concr. The place where a word or letter has been erased
or obliterated.
    Mod. The word was written over an erasure.
Total destruction; 'wiping out'. *rare.*
1794 GIBBON (O.) Erasure of cities. **1851 D WILSON**
Preh. Ann. II.iv.iv. 267 Repeated destruction of the settle-
ments and erasure of the accompanying progress of arts.

FOX

Reynard was playing mole tennis, singles,
laconically in the swamp. So far from barking
"clear and cold," like foxes in the dingles
of Fern Hill, he rasped out not I'm Croaking
but You Beware of Me.

I don't mean the dingles, I mean the hills.
You Beware of Me, he rasped, Reynard, fox populi:
Oh sleepless mole, danger makes the long peep
you make. All the red fox's food is red (there is so little
blue food). Beset, he might eat elderberries
in a pinch, though.
                     Now please listen to this Audubon fact:
Arctic fox are blue in summer, while the red's
rufous pelt is always shot through with gray.
It's the frog who will croak—Croak Monsieur—
not the fox, who will get him and others.

Foxing mars the columns of the tome
where I located this baleful information:
Satan materialized before a Connecticut child
in Branford, in fact, "in the shape of a fox," and tormented him.
It was Puritan Branford where all the proverbial grapes
lay falling or fallen drying themselves into raisins
in the fecund and dark swamp harvest when the fox still goes to his earths early.

SONG

White people pretending, black
people pretending to be Indians,
Indians pretending to be Sam Adams,
Sam Adams pretending to be beer.

Catholic teens pretending to be Hoosiers
pretending to reside in the Commonwealth
of Pennsylvania. Peppercorns pretending to be

      dollhouse doorknobs pretending to be artichokes;
      artichokes pretending to be doorknobs.

ISBNs pretending to be your social, zip
codes pretending and atomic numbers
pretending to be fake IDs. A meaty urologist
pretending to be the superb owl.

Radicals masquerading as framers,
farmers masquerading as physiocrats,
Sephardim acting like seraphim.

      Kimchee pretending to be leftover coleslaw;
      Boleslaw pretending to rhyme with the latter.

DOVE

While the Mandan Indians
were talking angrily with Mr. Chardon,
he sitting with his arms on a table between them,
a Dove, being pursued by a Hawk,
flew in through the open door,
and sat panting and worn out on Mr. Chardon's arm
for more than a minute, when it flew off.

After the Dove had escaped the Hawk
(the Dove sitting in the room panting and worn out near the Mandan Indians),
Mr. Chardon sat with his arms on a table.
His two feet were on the floor.

While Mr. Chardon sat angrily talking with the Mandan Indians,
the Dove flew in through the open door
by using its wings.
His arm attached at the shoulder,
Mr. Chardon could hear the voices of the Indians and could see them.

For more than a minute
the Dove sat panting and worn out on the arm.
The arm was Mr. Chardon's.
The Mandan Indians and Mr. Chardon were angry.
At the end of the arm was a hand.

The Dove used its talons to clutch the arm.

The people expressed their anger with voices and gestures.

The Hawk pursued the Dove, who flew in through the door.

The Hawk flew off.

Mr. Chardon's arms were on the table.

Talk was angry. The Hawk was a bird.

The spell of the Dove on the arm was longer than a minute.

The door was open, and Mr. Chardon was sitting at the table.

The Dove was panting and worn out.

The Mandan Indians were angry, and spoke as such.

They sat at the table with Mr. Chardon in the room.

The Hawk pursued the Dove.

The arm was clutched by the Dove.

Mr. Chardon sat at the table.

The Dove flew off with its wings.

The arm was under the Dove. The Dove was a bird.

Mr. Chardon and the Mandan Indians were people.

The latter could hear the former.

The emotional quality was anger.

The table had four legs. And so did each chair.

A PARALLELOGRAM

TO quote Rabbi Heschel, "To pray is to dream in league with God."

When we PRAY we're living in two time zones simultaneously:

the first of course IS Greenwich Mean Time, a factitious and endearing

place to call home, or TO call home from, since home is also

Zone 2, eternity, in which we DREAM of Zone 1. Furthermore,

"God's love is horizontal, like the INternet," wrote James

Gaillol, a bishop in France, which was a LEAGUE of Nations

founder and the home of St. Joan. So you might say WITH George

Herbert (in his poem "Col. 33:3"), "Our lives are hid with Christ in GOD."

#78 a & b. While the subject of #38—*Mrs. Fafnir Blenkinsop* (1942)—in which the gloves seem to be a food of straw, linsey-woolsey (pokeweed dye), and mustard seed, is seated at the spinet in a pose traditionally connected with St. Cecilia (as Anguissola), still #14 shows Dr. Blenkinsop reading to his bride from the Elder Edda, with their daughter (Postlethwaite?) on the left, an installation. "Of course, of course," Mrs. B. bursts out. "I always wondered why *Little House on the Prairie* sounded so much like Hemingway. Rose Wilder Lane went and redacted the story, and that's why! She and Hemingway were both journalists!" Where were we? #78 a & b. Fetch the waybread from your moosefoot wall pocket. *O esca viatorum!* Untie the wattled cotes. Adorn your temple with the speech-belt for a slide tour, a tour slide of the contact zone event. The speech-belt seems to be a food of snow.

DRESS PATTERN WITH AN INTERIOR: "Peace has the human dress" is line 12 of Blake's song of innocence, "The Divine Image."

A DANCE: *Bouki fait gumbo, lapin mangé li* is a Creole proverb. The Knopf book was published in 1969. Most material in the poem comes from lectures on the American frontier by Joyce E. Chaplin (lines 1–6, 12–14, and 20). "God gives, but He doesn't share" is a Haitian proverb cited by Paul Farmer in Tracy Kidder's book *Mountains Beyond Mountains* (Random House, 2004).

ANDIRONS: Lines 25–26 from *New England Begins: The Seventeenth Century*, Jonathan L. Fairbanks, Curator (Museum of Fine Arts, Boston, 1983).

SESTINA AT YIN YU TANG: Nancy W. Berliner, *Yin Yu Tang: The Architecture and Daily Life of a Chinese House* (Tuttle Publishing, 2003). Yin Yu Tang, an eighteenth-century Chinese house, was bought by the Peabody-Essex Museum in Salem, Massachusetts, and reassembled there with the guidance of the Huang family. "The snow will bring the world indoors" is from Sean O'Brien, "Blizzard," *Times Literary Supplement* 19 May 2006.

A LOT OF THE DAYS I WAKE UP: T. H. Breen, *The Marketplace of Revolution: How Consumer Politics Shaped American Independence* (Oxford University Press, 2004).

NERF: Line 4: Alex Preminger et al., eds., *Princeton Encyclopedia of Poetry and Poetics* (Princeton University Press, 1974). Line 10: John Hollander, *Rhyme's Reason: A Guide to English Verse* (Yale University Press, 1989). Lines 47–48: Ella Fitzgerald interview at www.pbs.org/wnet/americanmasters.

SPINOZA is a translation (first published in *Circumference* 2/1 Spring/Summer 2005) of this 1964 Borges sonnet:

> Las traslúcidas manos del judio
> Labran en la penumbra los cristales
> Y la tarde que mueres es miedo frío.
> (Las tardes a las tardes son iguales.)

Las monos y el espacio de jacinto
Que palidece en el confín del Ghetto
Casi no existen para el hombre quieto
Que está soñando un claro laberinto.
No lo turba la fama, ese reflejo
De sueños en el sueño de otro espejo,
Ni el temoroso amor de las doncellas.
Libre de la metáfora y del mito
Labra un arduo crystal: el infinito
Mapa de Aquel que es todas Sus estrellas.

FACE-MASQUE: "unedited . . ." —Annie Dillard, "Seeing," *Pilgrim at Tinker Creek* (Harper's Magazine Press, 1974). The Ashbery quotation "I think all . . ." is from *A Wave* (Farrar, Straus and Giroux, 1984). "I can think . . .": Virginia Woolf, *The Waves* (Hogarth Press, 1931). "On Tristan we . . .": "The World's Loneliest Dialect (Tristan da Cunha)," Walt Wolfram and Ben Ward, eds., *American Voices: How Dialects Differ from Coast to Coast* (Blackwell Publishing Limited, 2006). "The islanders on . . .": "Tristan da Cunha," *Encyclopedia Britannica* 11th Ed. (1911). "Newes . . .": Quoted in Matthew Mulcahy, *Hurricanes and Society in the British Greater Caribbean, 1624-1783* (The Johns Hopkins University Press, 2005). "Newton's particles of light . . .": William Blake, "Mock on, Mock on, Voltaire, Rousseau," lines 10–11.

DOVE: Lines 1–6: John James Audubon, *Writings and Drawings* (Library of America, 1999).

ACKNOWLEDGMENTS

"Sestina at Yin Yu Tang": *American Poet*

"Goth Plaint": *Black Clock*

"My Husband Sat Up": *Boston Review*

"It Was Christmas," "Oh," and "Fox": *Cincinnati Review*

"Spinoza": *Circumference*

"A Dance": *Fence*

"The Owl and the Lark," "Who'll Buy": *Fulcrum*

"Andirons," "Dove," "Hooke's Law," "Line Poem,"
and "Oldest Dog": *Hanging Loose*

"Salad": *jubilat*

"Dreyken" and "Song": *LIT*

"Coordinates": *New American Writing*

"Canzone delle Preposizioni" and "The Title": *A Public Space*

"Quaker Guns": *Times Literary Supplement*

"Text Panel": *TriQuarterly*

"We Beheld Two Nebulas:" and "Face-Masque": *Windsor Review*

"Dress Pattern with an Interior": *Yale Review*

"Wind Turbine": *Where the Road Begins: An Anthology of
Regional Writers* (The Cultural Organization of Lowell, 2007)

An Individual Artist Grant for Poetry from the Massachusetts Cultural Council (2006–2007) provided support to write this book. Many, many thanks to Matthew Zapruder, Joshua Beckman, and Lori Shine, its gracious editors, and to Jeff Clark of Quemadura, its gracious designer.